Elisha Brown

Victoria 1000 X 5
Children's Book Recycling Project

Did you know? Creating the habit of nightly bedtime reading "adds up" to this: By the time your child enters school, he or she will hear stories from 1000 books or more! Read to your child each day and begin literacy development, a stronger connection to you, and a lifetime love of books.

Please accept this gift of a book as a reminder of the importance of reading to young children and help support our goal—that all children in Victoria will have at least a thousand books read to them before they enter Kindergarten.

The *Victoria "1000 X 5" Children's Book Recycling Project* is a partnership among Success by 6®, South Vancouver Island; Greater Victoria School District #61 and Saanich Neighbourhood Place.

BEST
Nursery
Rhymes

Illustrated by Peter Stevenson

Ward Lock Limited · London

Little Bo-peep

Little Bo-peep has lost her sheep,
And can't tell where to find them;
Leave them alone, and they'll come home,
And bring their tails behind them.

Little Bo-peep fell fast asleep,
And dreamt she heard them bleating;
But when she awoke, she found it a joke,
For they were still a-fleeting.

Then up she took her little crook,
Determined for to find them;
She found them indeed, but it made her heart bleed,
For they'd left their tails behind them.

It happened one day, as Bo-peep did stray
Over a meadow hard by,
That there she espied their tails side by side,
All hung on a tree to dry.

She heaved a sigh, and wiped her eye,
And over the hills went rambling,
And tried what she could, as a shepherdess should,
To tack each again to its lambkin.

Poor Cock Robin

Who killed Cock Robin?
I, said the Sparrow,
With my bow and arrow,
I killed Cock Robin.

Who saw him die?
I, said the Fly,
With my little eye,
I saw him die.

Who caught his blood?
I, said the Fish,
With my little dish,
I caught his blood.

Who'll make the shroud?
I, said the Beetle,
With my thread and needle,
I'll make the shroud.

Who'll dig his grave?
I, said the Owl,
With my pick and shovel,
I'll dig his grave.

Who'll be the parson?
I, said the Rook,
With my little book,
I'll be the parson.

Who'll be the clerk?
I, said the Lark,
If it's not in the dark,
I'll be the clerk.

Who'll carry the link?
I, said the Linnet,
I'll fetch it in a minute,
I'll carry the link.

Who'll be chief mourner?
I, said the Dove,
I mourn for my love,
I'll be chief mourner.

Who'll carry the coffin?
I, said the Kite,
If it's not through the night,
I'll carry the coffin.

Who'll bear the pall?
We, said the Wren,
Both the cock and the hen,
We'll bear the pall.

Who'll sing a psalm?
I, said the Thrush,
As she sat on a bush,
I'll sing a psalm.

Who'll toll the bell?
I, said the Bull,
Because I can pull,
I'll toll the bell.

All the birds of the air
Fell a-sighing and a-sobbing,
When they heard the bell toll
For poor Cock Robin.

Pease pudding

Pease pudding hot,
Pease pudding cold,
Pease pudding in the pot,
Nine days old.

Some like it hot,
Some like it cold,
Some like it in the pot,
Nine days old.

Tweedle-dum and Tweedle-dee

Tweedle-dum and Tweedle-dee
Resolved to have a battle,
For Tweedle-dum said Tweedle-dee
Had spoiled his nice new rattle.
Just then flew by a monstrous crow,
As big as a tar-barrel,
Which frightened both the heroes so,
They quite forgot their quarrel.

11

Pussy in the well

Ding, dong, bell,
Pussy's in the well.
Who put her in?
Little Tommy Green.
Who pulled her out?
Little Tommy Stout.
What a naughty boy was that
To drown poor pussy cat.
Who never did him any harm,
But killed the mice in father's barn.

The old woman who lived in a shoe

There was an old woman who lived in a shoe;
She had so many children she didn't know what to do.
She gave them some broth without any bread;
Then whipped them all soundly and put them to bed.

Three blind mice

Three blind mice, three blind mice,
See how they run! See how they run!

They all ran after the farmer's wife,
Who cut off their tails with a carving knife.

Did ever you see such a thing in your life
As three blind mice?

Where, oh where?

Oh where, oh where has my little dog gone?
Oh where, oh where can he be?
With his ears cut short and his tail cut long,
Oh where, oh where is he?

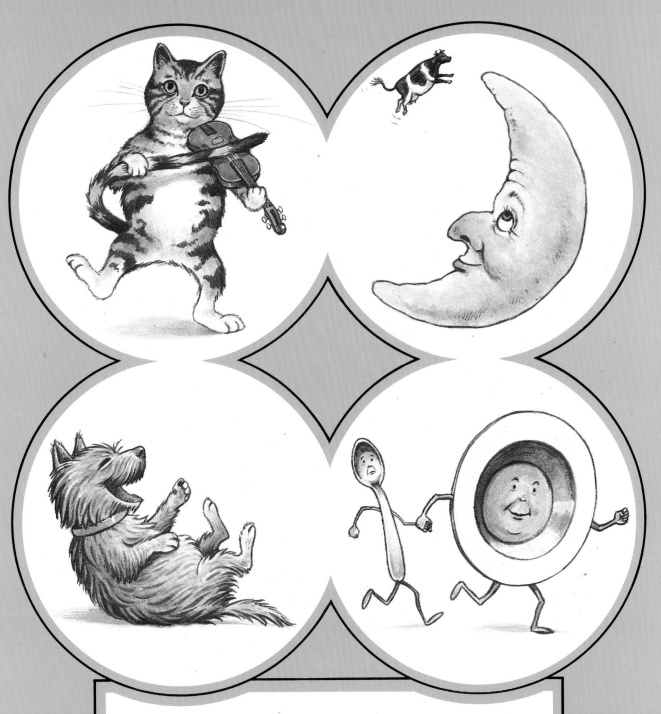

Hey, diddle, diddle

Hey, diddle, diddle, the cat and the fiddle,
The cow jumped over the moon;
The little dog laughed to see such sport,
And the dish ran away with the spoon.

The red sky

A red sky in the morning
Is the shepherd's warning;
A red sky at night
Is the shepherd's delight.

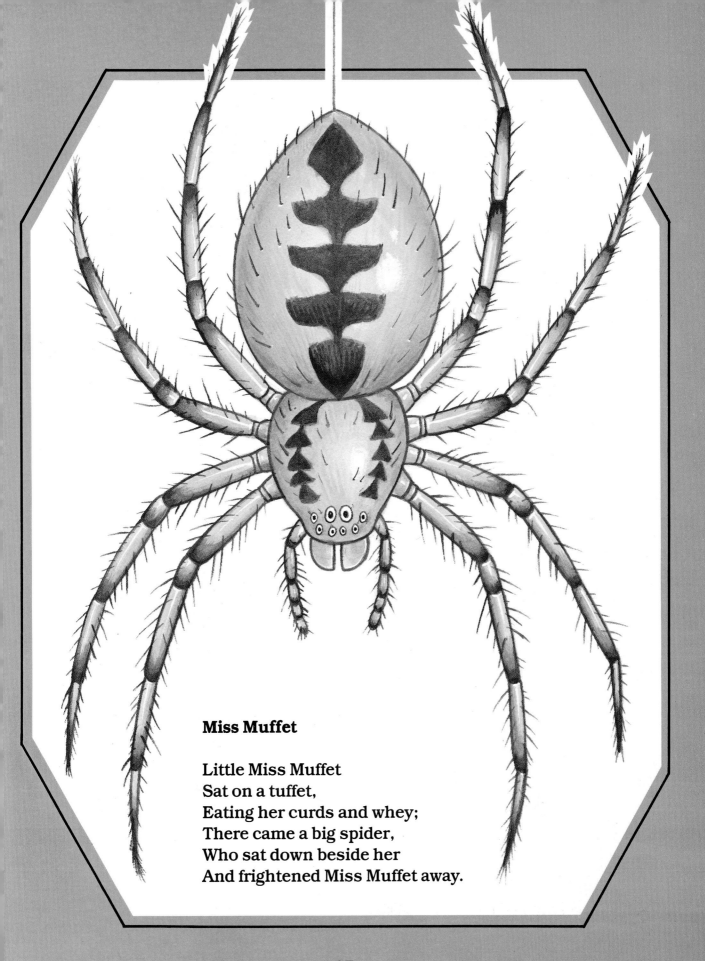

Miss Muffet

Little Miss Muffet
Sat on a tuffet,
Eating her curds and whey;
There came a big spider,
Who sat down beside her
And frightened Miss Muffet away.

Poor robin

The north wind doth blow,
And we shall have snow,
And what will poor robin do then?
Poor thing,
He'll sit in a barn,
And keep himself warm,
And hide his head under his wing.
Poor thing.

Christmas is coming

Christmas is coming, the geese are getting fat,
Please to put a penny in the old man's hat;
If you haven't got a penny, a ha'penny will do,
If you haven't got a ha'penny, God bless you.

The little black dog

The little black dog ran round the house,
And set the bull a-roaring,
And drove the monkey in the boat,
Who set the oars a-rowing,
And scared the cock upon the rock,
Who cracked his throat with crowing.

Tommy Tucker

Little Tommy Tucker,
Sings for his supper:
What shall we give him?
White bread and butter.
How shall he cut it
Without any knife?
How shall he marry
Without any wife?

The courting frog

A frog he would a-wooing go,
Heigh ho! says Rowley,
A frog he would a-wooing go,
Whether his mother would let him or no.
With a rowley, powley, gammon and spinach,
Heigh ho! says Anthony Rowley.

So off he set with his opera hat,
Heigh ho! says Rowley,
So off he set with his opera hat,
And on the road he met with a rat.
With a rowley, powley …

Pray, Mister Rat, will you go with me?
Heigh ho! says Rowley,
Pray, Mister Rat, will you go with me,
Kind Mrs. Mousey for to see?
With a rowley, powley …

They came to the door of Mousey's hall,
Heigh ho! says Rowley,
They gave a loud knock, and they gave a loud call.
With a rowley, powley…

Pray, Mrs. Mouse, are you within?
Heigh ho! says Rowley,
Oh yes, kind sirs, I'm sitting to spin.
With a rowley, powley…

Pray, Mrs. Mouse, will you give us some beer?
Heigh ho! says Rowley,
For Froggy and I are fond of good cheer.
With a rowley, powley...

Pray, Mr. Frog, will you give us a song?
Heigh ho! says Rowley,
Let it be something that's not very long.
With a rowley, powley...

Indeed, Mrs. Mouse, replied Mr. Frog,
Heigh ho! says Rowley,
A cold has made me as hoarse as a dog.
With a rowley, powley...

Since you have a cold, Mr. Frog, Mousey said,
Heigh ho! says Rowley,
I'll sing you a song that I have just made.
With a rowley, powley...

But while they were all a-merry-making,
Heigh ho! says Rowley,
A cat and her kittens came tumbling in.
With a rowley, powley...

The cat she seized the rat by the crown,
Heigh ho! says Rowley,
The kittens they pulled the little mouse down.
With a rowley, powley...

This put Mr. Frog in a terrible fright,
Heigh ho! says Rowley,
He took up his hat and he wished them good-night.
With a rowley, powley...

But, as Froggy was crossing over a brook,
Heigh ho! says Rowley,
A lily-white duck came and gobbled him up.
With a rowley, powley...

So there was an end of one, two, three,
Heigh ho! says Rowley,
The rat, the mouse, and the little frog-ee.
With a rowley, powley...

The pig and the hog

To market, to market, to buy a fat pig,
Home again, home again, jiggety-jig;
To market, to market, to buy a fat hog,
Home again, home again, jiggety-jog.

John Peel

Do ye ken John Peel, with his coat so grey,
Do ye ken John Peel, at the break of day,
Do ye ken John Peel when he's far, far away,
With his hounds and his horn in the morning.

'Twas the sound of his horn called me from my bed,
And the cry of his hounds has me oft-times led.
For Peel's 'view halloo' would waken the dead,
Or a fox from his lair in the morning.

Do ye ken John Peel with his hounds so true,
Ranter and Ringwood, Bellman and Blue,
From a find to a check, from a check to a view,
From a view to a death in the morning.

The stolen tarts

The Queen of Hearts
She made some tarts,
All on a summer's day;

The Knave of Hearts
He stole the tarts,
And took them clean away.

The King of Hearts
Called for the tarts,
And beat the Knave full sore;

The Knave of Hearts
Brought back the tarts,
And vowed he'd steal no more.

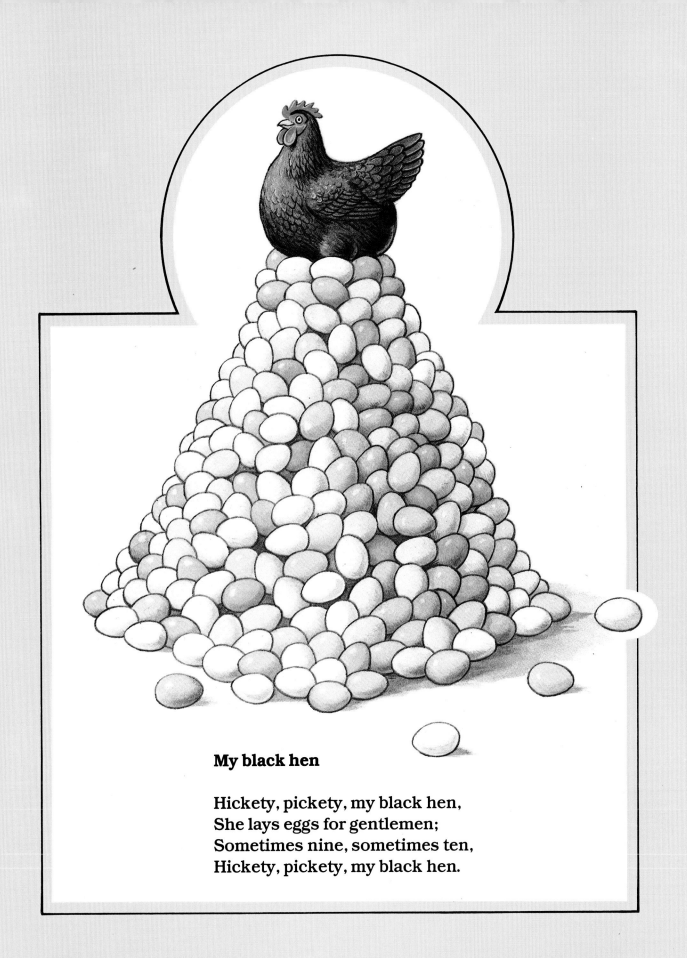

My black hen

Hickety, pickety, my black hen,
She lays eggs for gentlemen;
Sometimes nine, sometimes ten,
Hickety, pickety, my black hen.

Jacky

See-saw, Margery Daw,
Jacky shall have a new master;
And he shall have but a penny a day,
Because he can't work any faster.

The tickling rhyme

Round and round the garden
Like a teddy bear;
One step, two step,
Tickle you under there!

The little hobby horse

I had a little hobby horse
And it was dapple grey,
Its head was made of pea-straw,
Its tail was made of hay.

I sold him to an old woman
For a copper groat,
And I'll not sing my song again
Without a new coat.

The lion and the unicorn

The lion and the unicorn
Fought for the crown;
The lion beat the unicorn
Up and down the town.
Some gave them white bread,
And some gave them brown,
Some gave them plum cake
And sent them out of town.

A crooked man

There was a crooked man, and he walked a crooked mile,
He found a crooked sixpence against a crooked stile:
He bought a crooked cat, which caught a crooked mouse,
And they all lived together in a little crooked house.

The cock crows

The cock crows in the morn
To tell us all to rise,
And he that lies late
Will never be wise:
For early to bed,
And early to rise,
Makes a man healthy
And wealthy and wise.

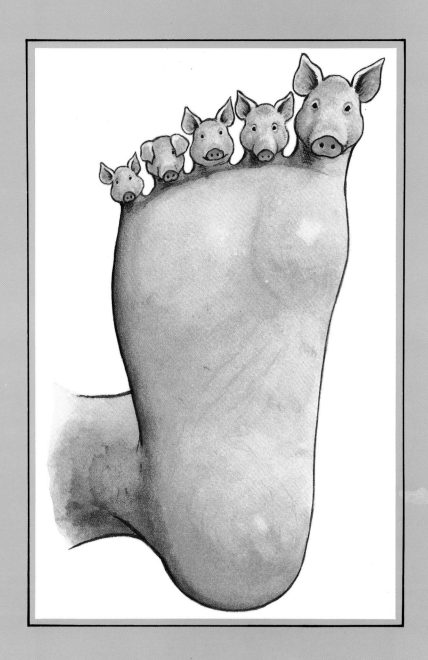

Five little piggies

This little pig went to market;
This little pig stayed at home;
This little pig had roast beef;
This little pig had none;
This little pig cried 'Wee, wee, wee!'
And ran all the way home.

Blackbird pie

Sing a song of sixpence,
A pocket full of rye;
Four-and-twenty blackbirds
Baked in a pie.

When the pie was opened,
The birds began to sing;
Was not that a dainty dish
To set before the King?

The King was in the counting-house,
Counting out his money;
The Queen was in the parlour,
Eating bread and honey;

The maid was in the garden,
Hanging out the clothes;
When down came a little bird
And pecked off her nose!

Doctor Foster

Doctor Foster went to Gloucester,
In a shower of rain;
He stepped in a puddle, up to the middle,
And never went there again.

Bandy legs

As I was going to sell my eggs,
I met a man with bandy legs,
Bandy legs and crooked toes,
I tripped up his heels, and he fell on his nose.

Hickory, dickory, dock

Hickory, dickory, dock,
The mouse ran up the clock;
The clock struck one,
The mouse ran down;
Hickory, dickory, dock.

Jack

Jack, be nimble,

Jack, be quick,

Jack, jump over the candlestick.

Humpty Dumpty

Humpty Dumpty sat on a wall,
Humpty Dumpty had a great fall.
All the King's horses,
And all the King's men,
Couldn't put Humpty together again.

Jack's house

This is the house that Jack built.
This is the malt
That lay in the house
That Jack built.

This is the rat
That ate the malt
That lay in the house
That Jack built.

This is the cat that killed the rat
That ate the malt
That lay in the house that Jack built.

This is the dog that worried the cat
That killed the rat that ate the malt
That lay in the house that Jack built.

This is the cow with the crumpled horn
That tossed the dog that worried the cat
That killed the rat that ate the malt
That lay in the house that Jack built.

This is the maiden all forlorn
That milked the cow with the crumpled horn
That tossed the dog that worried the cat
That killed the rat that ate the malt
That lay in the house that Jack built.

This is the man all tattered and torn
That kissed the maiden all forlorn
That milked the cow with the crumpled horn
That tossed the dog that worried the cat
That killed the rat that ate the malt
That lay in the house that Jack built.

This is the priest all shaven and shorn
That married the man all tattered and torn
That kissed the maiden all forlorn
That milked the cow with the crumpled horn
That tossed the dog that worried the cat
That killed the rat that ate the malt
That lay in the house that Jack built.

This is the cock that crowed in the morn
That waked the priest all shaven and shorn
That married the man all tattered and torn
That kissed the maiden all forlorn
That milked the cow with the crumpled horn
That tossed the dog that worried the cat
That killed the rat that ate the malt
That lay in the house that Jack built.

This is the farmer that sowed the corn
That fed the cock that crowed in the morn
That waked the priest all shaven and shorn
That married the man all tattered and torn
That kissed the maiden all forlorn
That milked the cow with the crumpled horn
That tossed the dog that worried the cat
That killed the rat that ate the malt
That lay in the house that Jack built.

King of the bush

Kookaburra sits in the old gum tree,
Merry, merry king of the bush is he,
Laugh kookaburra, laugh kookaburra,
Gay your life must be.

The flying pig

Dickory, dickory, dare,
The pig flew up in the air;
The man in brown soon brought him down,
Dickory, dickory, dare.

Baa, baa, black sheep

Baa, baa, black sheep, have you any wool?
Yes, sir; yes, sir, three bags full;
One for my master, one for my dame,
And one for the little boy who lives down the lane.

The kittens' mittens

Three little kittens they lost their mittens,
And they began to cry,
Oh, mother dear, we sadly fear
That we have lost our mittens.
What! lost your mittens, you naughty kittens!
Then you shall have no pie.
Mee-ow, mee-ow, mee-ow.
No, you shall have no pie.

The three little kittens they found their mittens,
And they began to cry,
Oh, mother dear, see here, see here,
For we have found our mittens.
Put on your mittens, you silly kittens,
And you shall have some pie.
Purr-r, purr-r, purr-r,
Oh, let us have some pie.

The three little kittens put on their mittens,
And soon ate up the pie;
Oh, mother dear, we greatly fear
That we have soiled our mittens.
What! soiled your mittens, you naughty kittens!
Then they began to sigh.
Meo-ow, mee-ow, mee-ow.
Then they began to sigh.

The three little kittens they washed their mittens,
And hung them out to dry;
Oh! mother dear, do you not hear
That we have washed our mittens?
What! washed your mittens, then you're good kittens,
But I smell a rat close by.
Mee-ow, mee-ow, mee-ow.
We smell a rat close by.

Simple Simon

Simple Simon met a pieman,
Going to the fair;
Says Simple Simon to the pieman,
Let me taste your ware.

Says the pieman to Simple Simon,
Show me first your penny;
Says Simple Simon to the pieman,
Indeed I have not any.

Simple Simon went a-fishing,
For to catch a whale;
All the water he had got
Was in his mother's pail.

Simple Simon went to look
If plums grew on a thistle;
He pricked his finger very much,
Which made poor Simon whistle.

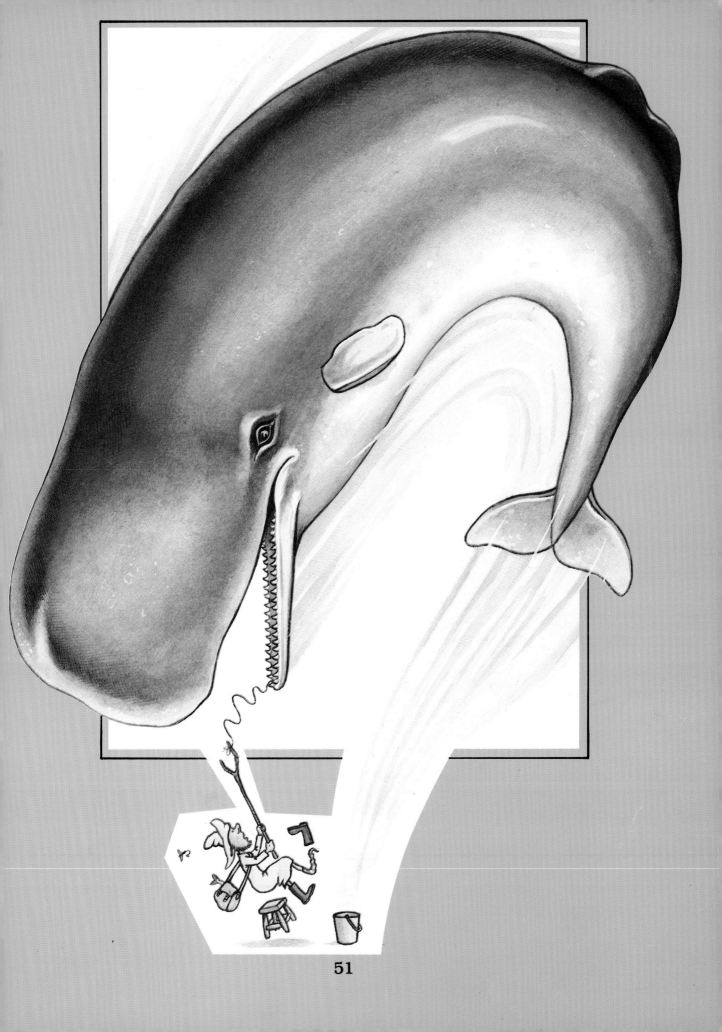

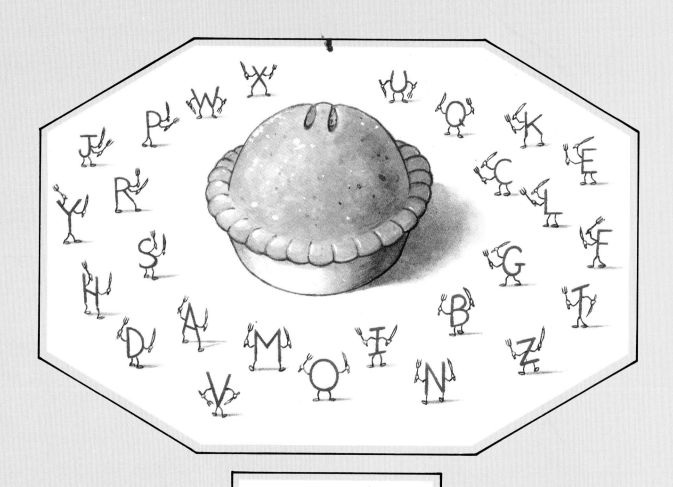

Alphabet pie

A was an apple pie;
B bit it,
C cut it,
D dealt it,
E eat it,
F fought for it,
G got it,
H had it,
I inspected it,
J jumped for it,
K kept it,
L longed for it,
M mourned for it,

N nodded at it,
O opened it,
P peeped in it,
Q quartered it,
R ran for it,
S stole it,
T took it,
U upset it,
V viewed it,
W wanted it,
X, Y, Z, and ampersand
All wished for a piece in hand.

Brushing the cobwebs off the sky!

There was an old woman tossed up in a basket,
Ninety times as high as the moon;
Where she was going, I couldn't but ask it,
For in her hand she carried a broom.

Old woman, old woman, old woman, quoth I,
O whither, O whither, O whither so high?
To brush the cobwebs off the sky!
Shall I go with thee?
Aye, bye and bye.

The man in the moon

The man in the moon
Came down too soon,
And asked his way to Norwich;
He went by the south,
And burnt his mouth
With supping cold plum porridge.

Mother Hubbard's dog

Old Mother Hubbard she went to the cupboard
To get her poor dog a bone,
But when she got there the cupboard was bare,
And so the poor dog had none.

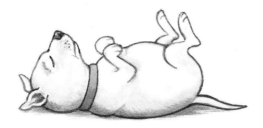

She went to the baker's
To buy him some bread;
But when she came back
The poor dog was dead.

She went to the joiner's
To buy him a coffin;
But when she came back
The poor dog was laughing.

She took a clean dish
To get him some tripe;
But when she came back
He was smoking a pipe.

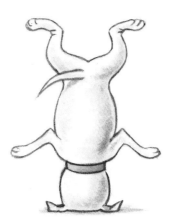

She went to the fishmonger's
To buy him some fish,
And when she came back
He was licking the dish.

She went to the tavern
For white wine and red;
But when she came back
The dog stood on his head.

She went to the hatter's
To buy him a hat;
But when she came back
He was feeding the cat.

She went to the barber's
To buy him a wig;
But when she came back
He was dancing a jig.

She went to the fruiterer's
To buy him some fruit;
But when she came back
He was playing the flute.

She went to the tailor's
To buy him a coat;
But when she came back
He was riding a goat.

She went to the cobbler's
To buy him some shoes;
But when she came back
He was reading the news.

She went to the seamstress
To buy him some linen;
But when she came back
The dog was spinning.

The dame made a curtsey,
The dog made a bow;
The dame said, 'Your servant,'
The dog said, 'Bow, wow!'

Barber, barber

Barber, barber, shave a pig,
How many hairs will make a wig?
Four and twenty, that's enough.
Give the barber a pinch of snuff.

The moon and me

I see the moon,
And the moon sees me;
God bless the moon,
And God bless me.

Index of First Lines

© Ward Lock Limited 1982, 1984

First published in Great Britain in 1984
by Ward Lock Limited, 82 Gower Street,
London WC1E 6EQ, a Pentos Company.

Text filmset in Bookman
by Text Filmsetters of Orpington, Kent
Printed and bound in Belgium.

British Library Cataloguing in Publication Data

Nursery rhymes.
  1. Nursery rhymes, English
  I. Stevenson, Peter
  398'.8   PZ8.3

  ISBN 0-7063-6296-9

The lucky pin

See a pin and pick it up,
All the day you'll have good luck;
See a pin and let it lay,
Bad luck you'll have all the day.